How have things changed?

People Who Help Us

James Nixon

First published in 2008 by
Franklin Watts
338 Euston Road
London NW1 3BH

Franklin Watts Australia
Level 17/207 Kent Street
Sydney NSW 2000

ISBN: 978 0 7496 7847 0

Dewey classification number: 331.7′1

A CIP catalogue record for this book is available from the British Library.

Planning and production by Discovery Books Limited
Editor: James Nixon
Designer: Rob Norridge

Photographs: p6 Reg Speller/Getty Images, p7 Chris Fairclough, p8 (top) Mary Evans Picture Library, p8 (bottom) Science and Society Picture Library, p9 Chris Fairclough, p10 (top) Mary Evans Picture Library, p10 (bottom) Science and Society Picture Library, p11 Chris Fairclough, p12 F.G. Weller/Getty Images, p13 Chris Fairclough, p14 (top) Courtesy of The Royal Veterinary College, p14 (bottom) Mary Evans Picture Library, p15 Chris Fairclough, p16 Mary Evans Picture Library, p17 Chris Fairclough, p18 Mary Evans Picture Library, p19 Chris Fairclough, p20 (top) Topham Picture Point, p20 (bottom) Milton Keynes Museum, p21 Chris Fairclough, p22 Courtesy of Nottinghamshire County Council and www.picturethepast.org.uk, p23 Bobby Humphrey, p24 The British Postal Museum & Archive, p25 (top) Chris Fairclough, p25 (middle, bottom) The British Postal Museum & Archive, p26 Beamish Museum, Photographic Archive, p27 (top) Bobby Humphrey, p27 (middle) Chris Fairclough, p27 (bottom) Bobby Humphrey.

Cover photos: (top) Mary Evans Picture Library, (bottom) Chris Fairclough.

Printed in China

Franklin Watts is a division of Hachette Children's Books, an Hachette Livre UK company.
www.hachettelivre.co.uk

Contents

How has work changed? 6
The doctor 8
The nurse 10
The dentist 12
The vet 14
The police 16
The firefighter 18
The teacher 20
The librarian 22
The postal worker 24
The refuse collector 26
Glossary 28
Further information 29
Index 30

How has work changed?

For hundreds of years people have worked to help others. Doctors have cured our illnesses. Postal workers have delivered letters. The police have made sure the law is obeyed.

Over the years the methods, **technology** and equipment that these workers use has changed.

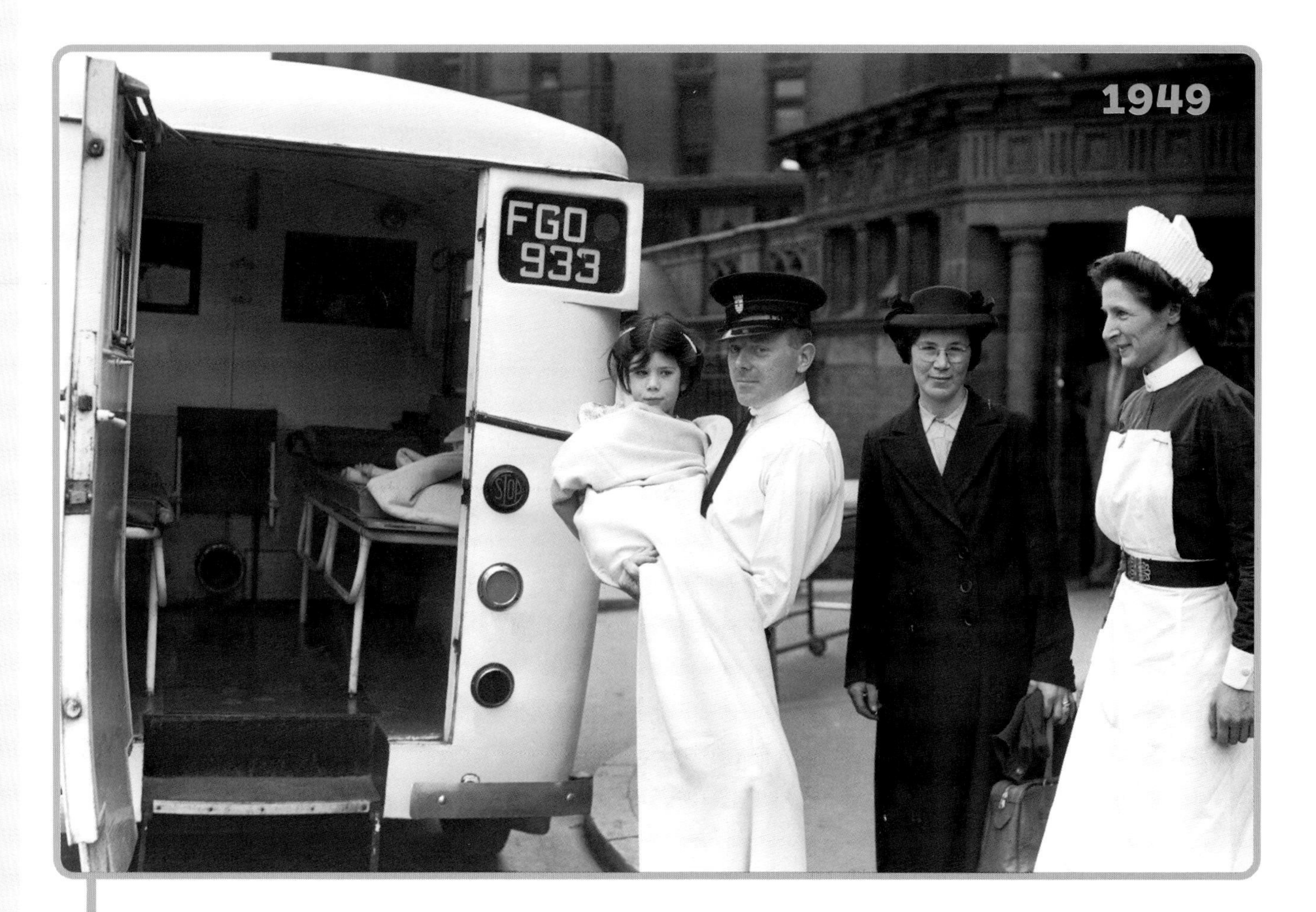

An ambulance worker's job in the 1940s was to drive sick people to hospital. They did not have equipment to treat people in the ambulance.

Today, the people who help us have better equipment than they did in the past. Modern ambulance workers carry a lot of **medical** instruments in their vehicle. This child (right) is being given some oxygen through a mask.

Then and now

Why is it easier to get patients into a modern ambulance?

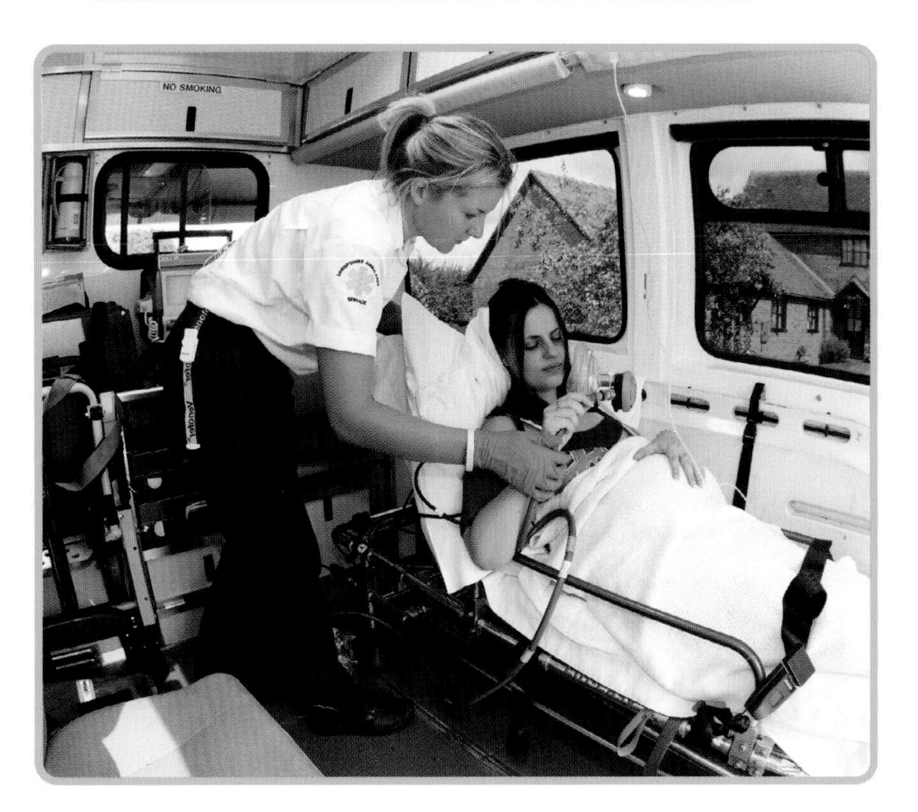

Workers are often more skilled than they were in the past. Ambulance workers are now medical experts who can treat people before they get to hospital.

The doctor

In the early part of the twentieth century most people rarely saw the doctor. The doctor was expensive and he was only called out if the illness was serious.

The doctor was nearly always a man. He would visit the house bringing his equipment with him. This picture shows a doctor on a home visit in 1940. He is using a **stethoscope** to listen to his patient's chest.

By the end of the 1940s it cost nothing to see the doctor. Most doctors had a **surgery** where people visited them.

Today, it still costs nothing to see the doctor. You can visit him or her whenever you feel unwell.

Then and now

Compare this surgery to the one in the 1940s.

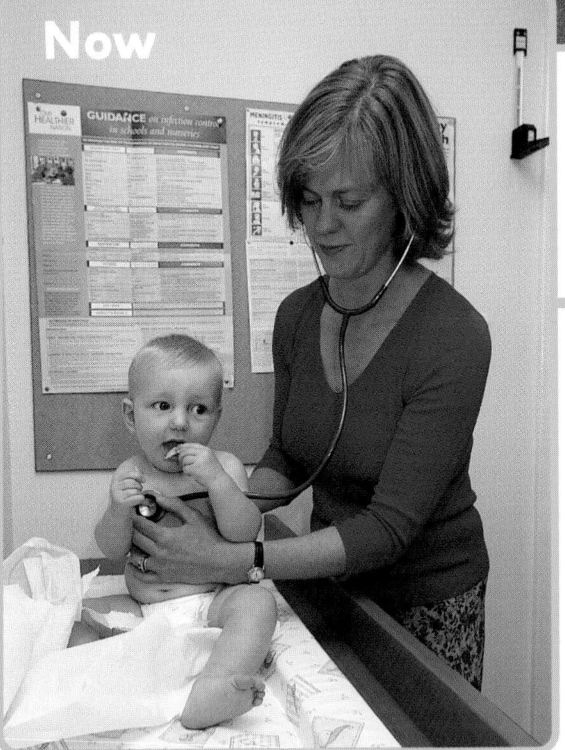

Doctors still use stethoscopes. However, new technology is being developed all the time. There are now many more instruments and medicines to treat people with.

Doctors also know much more about how our bodies work. Operations carried out by **surgeons** are more **effective** than they were in the past.

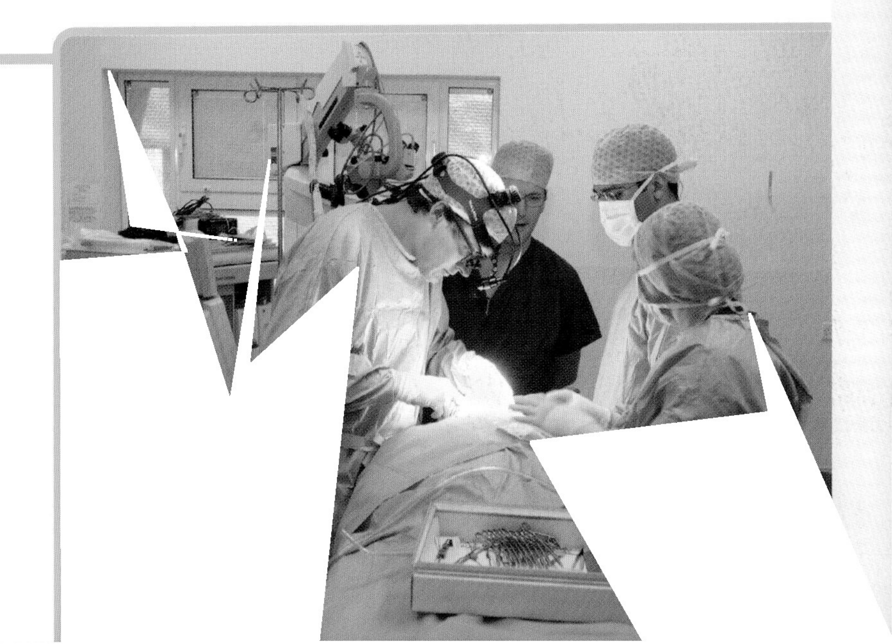

The nurse

A nurse's job was very different over a hundred years ago. They washed, fed and cared for the patients just like today. However, they also had to cook for patients and do the washing up themselves.

1905

Look at the picture of this nurse in 1905. Nurses wore a long skirt with a white apron.

Then and now

How do these clothes differ from the uniforms nurses wear today?

Look at this poster from the 1940s. Nursing was seen as a job for women at this time.

Today, nurses know much more about medicine. They can teach people how to look after themselves and stay healthy. They can also give patients advice about their illness. This nurse is taking an **x-ray** of a girl's broken leg.

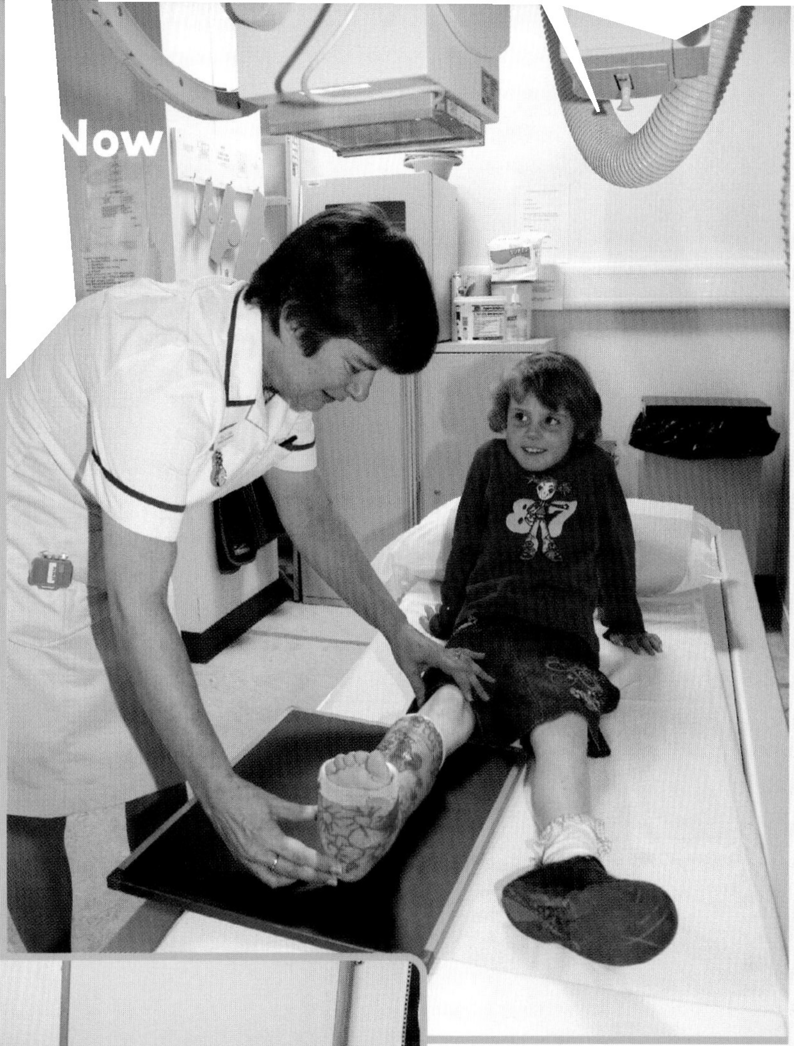

Now

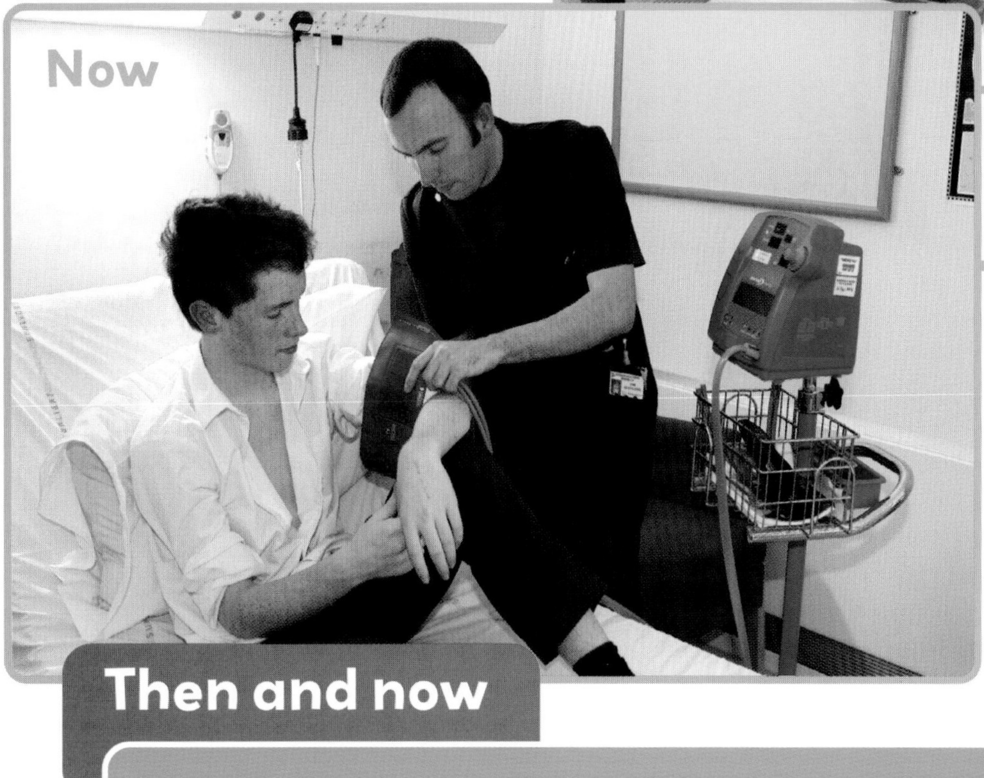

Now

Today, a man or woman can become a nurse.

Then and now

Nurses have more skills than they did in the past. They can now give injections. This male nurse is checking a patient's blood pressure.

The dentist

Until the middle of the twentieth century, only the very wealthy could afford to go to a proper dentist.

A dentist's methods could be very painful in the past. If the patient had a serious toothache the tooth was removed with brute force.

How is the dentist's assistant helping in this picture?

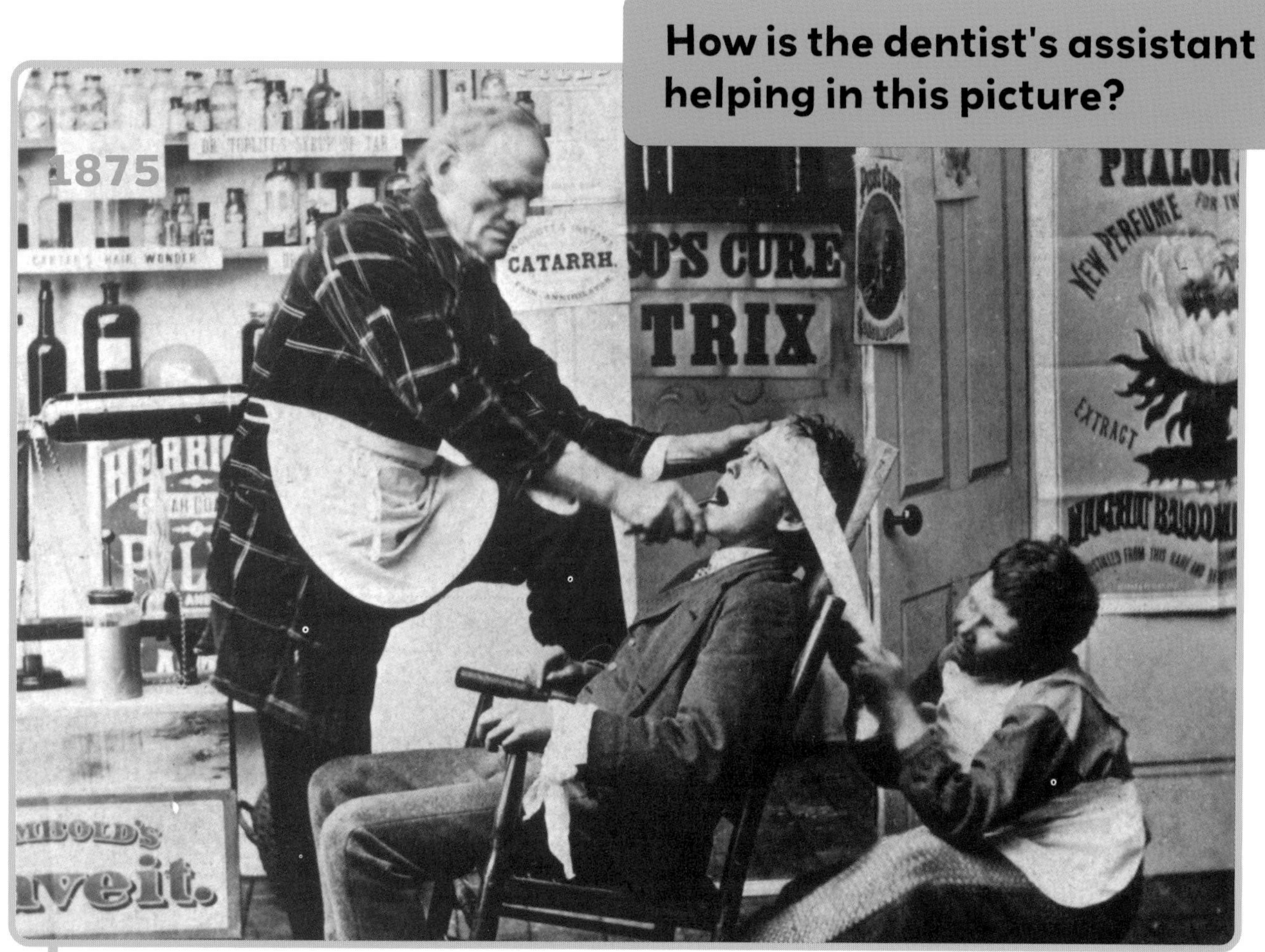

This picture shows a dentist in 1875. Patients sat on a wooden chair that had arms to grab on to when they felt the pain. Rotten teeth often needed pulling out, as most people did not brush their teeth at this time.

Today, most people visit their dentist for a regular check-up.

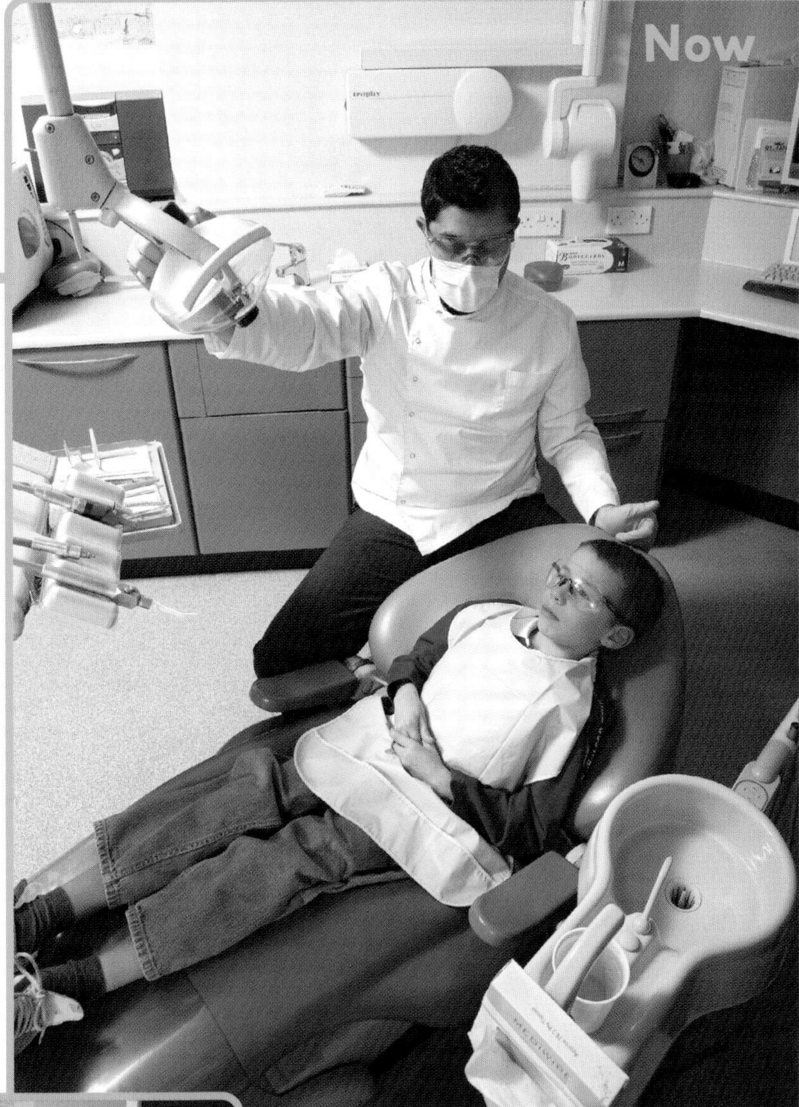

Look at this photo taken inside a modern dentist's surgery. The dentist has special drills to remove rotten parts of a tooth. **Anaesthetics** make treatment painless.

We now understand how to look after our teeth a lot better. This dentist is showing a child the correct way to brush.

The vet

Over a hundred years ago a vet's methods and instruments were very different.

There were no anaesthetics. Animals could be in a lot of pain during an operation. Look at this wooden operating table from the 1800s. It had clamps at both ends to hold the animal still.

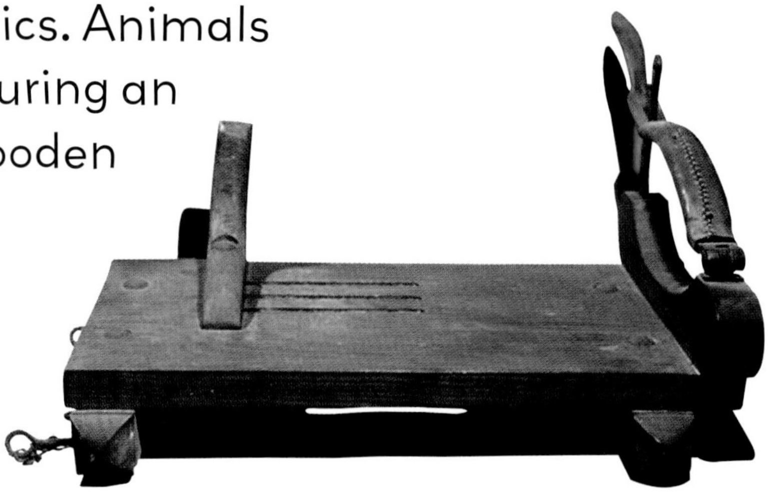

Eighty years ago vets worked mainly with farm animals. This vet is out on a farm taking an x-ray of a horse.

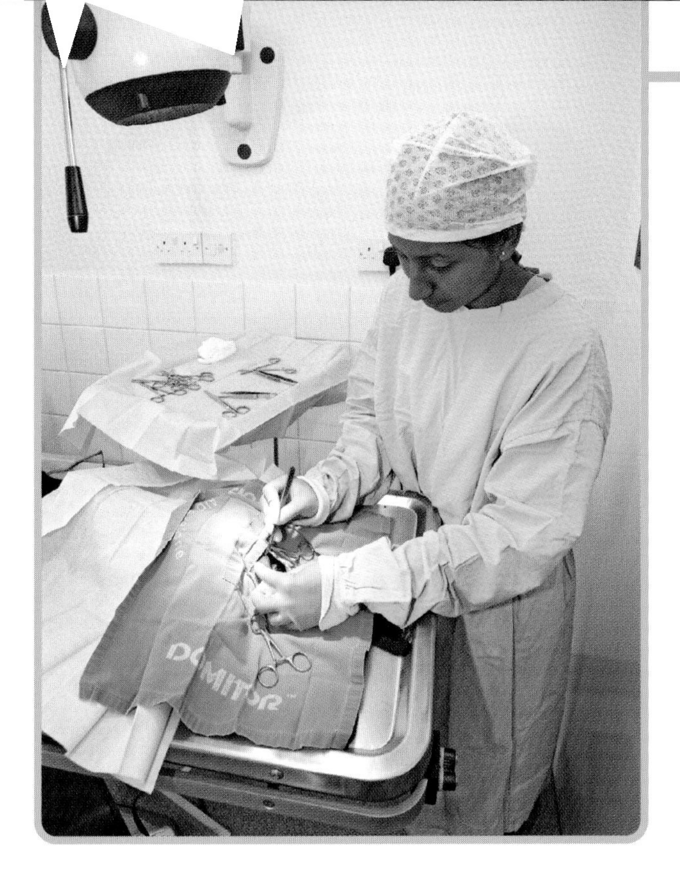

Today's vets are highly skilled. They have better equipment and treatments. Operations are usually painless and more likely to be a success.

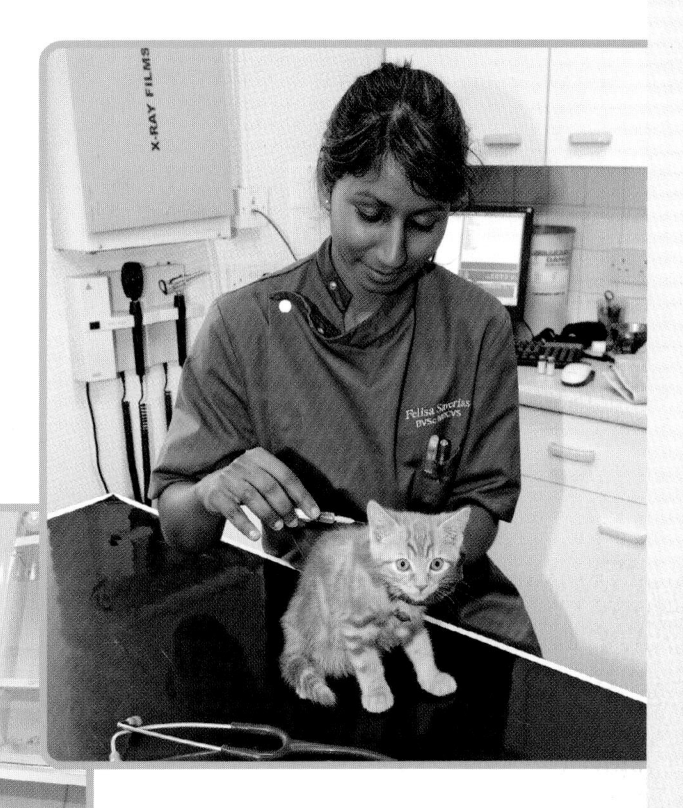

Vets still deal with farm animals, but nowadays they spend more time treating household pets.

Then and now

Vets treat many more different kinds of animals than in the past. Exotic creatures like snakes are often brought in as pets. This vet is clipping the nails of a tortoise.

The police

Over 50 years ago a police officer's uniform was a long coat with a high collar and a tall hat. This made it difficult for an officer to run quickly.

1956

Most police officers in the 1950s patrolled the streets on foot or on a bicycle. They carried a whistle in case they needed to call for help.

Then and now

Do you think it would be easier to catch a criminal then or now? Why?

A modern-day police officer can respond to **emergency** calls very quickly.

The police force have motorbikes, cars, boats and helicopters. Police officers now carry a radio to keep in contact with each other.

Now

Today's uniform protects them a lot better. Look at this police officer. She is putting a thick vest on to protect herself from injury.

The firefighter

A firefighter's uniform in 1900 was made of ordinary materials and could even catch fire. Dealing with fires was difficult as firefighters had less equipment than they do today.

Look at this old fire engine. It was not easy to get to a fire quickly with a horse and cart.

They did have a water pump on the back of the cart, and hoses. But firefighters could not always get into burning buildings, as they did not have masks or torches.

Look how the firemen are balanced on the sides of the cart. How would they feel rushing to a fire like this?

Look at these modern firefighters. The helmet and clothes protect them from the fire. Breathing equipment and torches help them go into smoke-filled buildings.

Fire engines now get firefighters to an emergency quickly. A long ladder on top of the engine helps them reach the tops of buildings.

Then and now

Make a list of reasons why firefighting is easier today.

Today, firefighters don't just put out fires. They also rescue people from collapsed buildings, floods and car accidents.

The teacher

A hundred years ago teachers were very strict, and most schoolchildren were very frightened of their teachers.

Then and now

Compare this classroom to your own classroom, and the room on the next page. How have classrooms changed?

1910

Pupils had to stay seated at their desks and be silent during lessons. Everybody faced the front, towards the teacher's desk. If the teacher spotted bad behaviour they could hit pupils with a cane (right) as punishment.

Today, lessons are a lot more friendly and relaxed. Classrooms can be noisy, busy places. The teacher goes around the room to help children with their work. Hitting schoolchildren is not allowed.

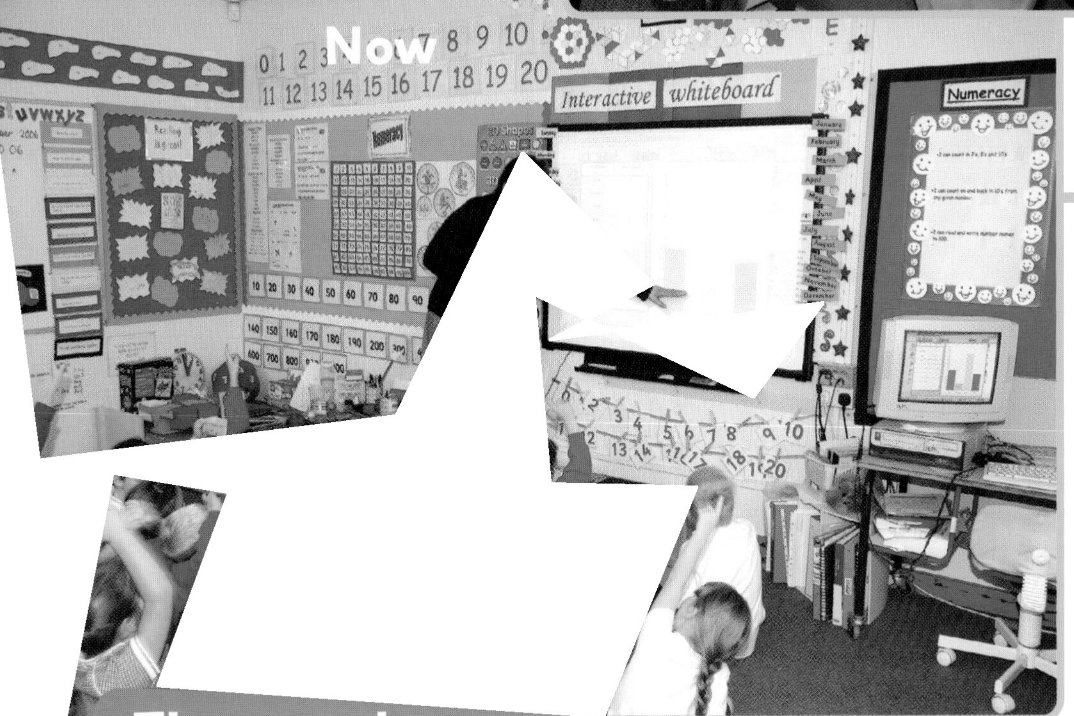

Teachers often get the pupils to sit on the carpet while they teach.

Then and now

Compare the pictures above to the lesson in 1910. Do you think school was more fun then or now?

The librarian

In some libraries 70 years ago you could not browse the shelves for a book. You asked the librarian for the book you wanted and he or she would go and get it.

What would the problems be with the old card system?

Look at this photo taken in the 1940s. The name of each book in a library then was written on a piece of card. Librarians checked these cards to find out where books were kept.

Now look inside this modern library. Today, librarians keep a record of all the books on a computer system. The librarian will help you find whatever you need, but you can browse the shelves yourself.

What problems can there be with a computer?

Nowadays libraries stock more than just books and maps. You can borrow music and films on CD, video and DVD. You can also search the **Internet** and read magazines.

The postal worker

For over a hundred years the railways were used to transport mail over long distances. Sorting the mail was done by hand on the train.

1930s

Then and now

Look at the clothes on the postal worker (below) and compare them to now. What differences can you see?

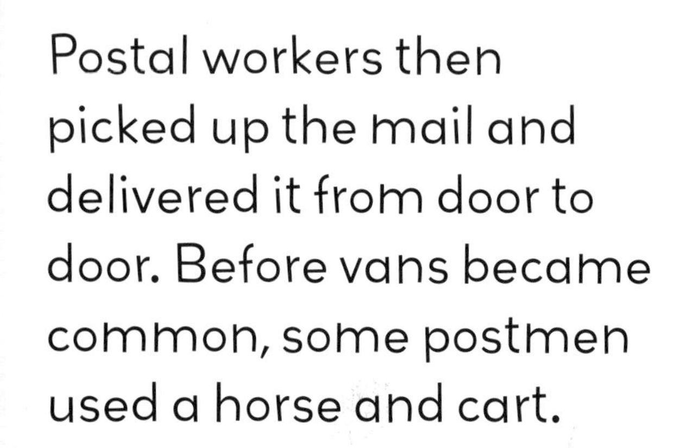

Postal workers then picked up the mail and delivered it from door to door. Before vans became common, some postmen used a horse and cart.

1894

I Certify that Mr. J C Poppleton's horse of the Post Office
is suffering from sore shoulders
and unable to perform his official duties.
He is to resume duty on or before the the 7th of November
or obtain a renewal of this Certificate.

Sick notes

Rushing around with the horse and cart was tough work. It was tough on the horse as well. Workers often had to write sick notes for their horses because they got sore shoulders.

Sorting the mail is now done automatically by a machine before it is transported by train or van. Letters can also be sent abroad by plane to anywhere in the world.

Then and now

In 2004 Royal Mail stopped sorting letters by hand on night trains. New hi-tech equipment can sort 30,000 letters an hour compared with just 3,000 on the night trains.

Today, a variety of vehicles are used by postal workers to do their rounds. In towns the **Royal Mail** is introducing small electric vans like this one. These are better for the **environment**.

A **quad bike** is being used to deliver the post on this **remote** Scottish island.

The refuse collector

In the 1920s most waste was collected by men in a horse-driven cart.

At this time there was less packaging so less was thrown away. Rubbish was usually taken away to a tip where it was often burnt. A lot of the waste produced then was ashes and dust from people's own fires. That's why refuse collectors were called dustmen.

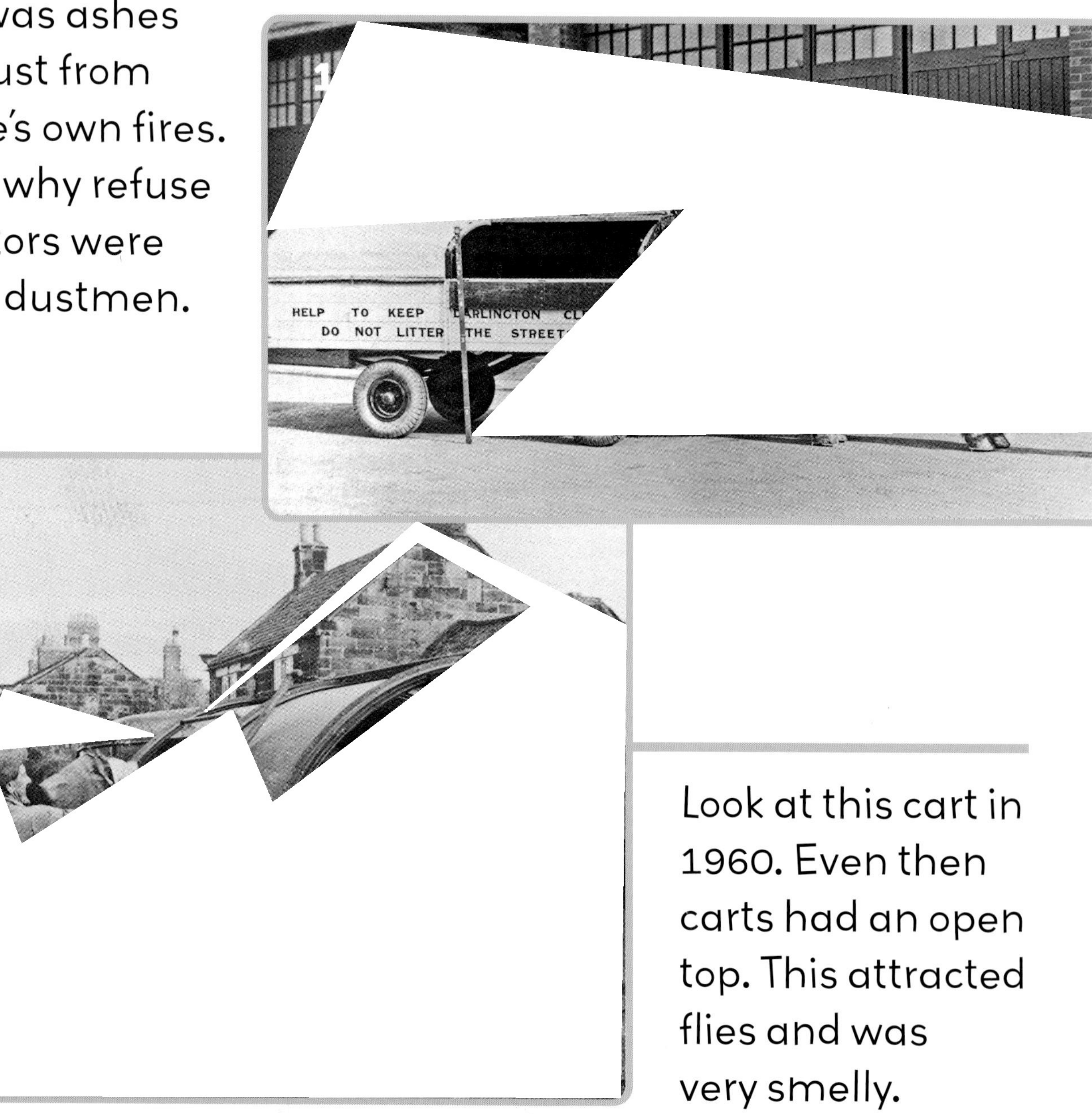

1960

Look at this cart in 1960. Even then carts had an open top. This attracted flies and was very smelly.

Today, we create more waste, but we try to recycle a lot more. These modern refuse collectors are picking up materials that have been sorted for recycling.

Each material is put into a different section of the truck. Look at all of these cans that have been collected.

Why do we not burn waste so much today?

Rubbish that is not recycled is taken to a massive dump called a **landfill**. It is taken in large refuse trucks like this one. Rubbish is squashed up at the back of the truck so it can be packed in tight.

Then and now

How is this modern refuse truck better than the old ones on the opposite page?

Glossary

Anaesthetics Drugs given to prevent you from feeling pain.

Effective If something is effective it produces a useful result.

Emergency A serious problem that must be dealt with quickly.

Environment The natural world around us.

Exotic Describes pets that are unusual and come from a far away country.

Internet The worldwide computer network that allows information to be exchanged from one person's computer to another.

Landfill A site where waste is dumped and buried in the ground.

Medical Relating to the treatment and prevention of illness and injuries.

Quad bike A motorcycle with four large tyres.

Remote Describes a place located far away from a town or city.

Royal Mail The main company in the UK that delivers the post.

Stethoscope A device used by doctors to listen to a patient's heart and breathing.

Surgeons Doctors who perform operations.

Surgery A room or building where doctors or dentists work.

Technology The use of science and machines to do practical things.

X-ray Pictures taken to examine the bones or organs inside a person's body.

Further information

Places to visit:

The Fire and Police Musuem (www.firepolicemuseum.org.uk)
The exhibits in this museum show how firefighters and police officers have worked throughout the ages.

British Dental Association Museum, London
(www.bda.org/museum/index.cfm)
In this museum find out how people have – or haven't – looked after their teeth in the past, and see the artefacts that dentists have used over the years.

Websites:

http://postalheritage.org.uk/exhibitions/movingthemail/
presents a detailed history of how postal workers have delivered the mail

www.ngfl-cymru.org.uk/vtc/nurses/eng/Introduction/default.htm
shows you the role of nurses today and in the past

Books to read:

Florence Nightingale (Ways into History), Sally Hewitt, 2004 (Franklin Watts)
Out and About series, Sue Barraclough, 2006 (Franklin Watts)
People Who Help Us (History from Photographs), Kathleen Cox and Pat Hughes, 2006 (Wayland)
People Who Help Us series, 2007 (Franklin Watts)
When I'm at Work series, Deborah Chancellor and Sue Barraclough, 2005 (Franklin Watts)
Where People Work (Where You Live), Ruth Nason, 2007 (Franklin Watts)

Index

ambulance workers 6-7
anaesthetics 13, 14

dentists 12-13
doctors 6, 8-9

fire engines 18-19
firefighters 18-19

librarians 22-23

medical equipment 6-9, 11, 13, 14-15
medicines 9, 11

nurses 10-11

operations 9, 14-15

police 6, 16-17
postal workers 6, 24-25

recycling 27
refuse collectors 26-27
refuse trucks 26-27

sorting letters 24-25
surgeries 8-9, 13, 15

teachers 20-21

uniforms 10, 16-17, 18-19, 24

vets 14-15

x-rays 11, 14